SERENA VS. VENUS

HOW A PHOTOGRAPH SPOTLIGHTED THE FIGHT FOR EQUALITY

by Danielle Smith-Llera

Content Adviser: Ben Rothenberg
Board Member
International Tennis Writers Association

COMPASS POINT BOOKS
a capstone imprint

Compass Point Books are published by Capstone,
1710 Roe Crest Drive, North Mankato, Minnesota 56003
www.mycapstone.com

Editor: Catherine Neitge
Designers: Tracy Davies McCabe and Catherine Neitge
Media Researcher: Eric Gohl
Library Consultant: Kathleen Baxter
Production Specialist: Laura Manthe

Image Credits
Getty Images: Bettmann, 21, 22, 23, 24, 39, Bob Thomas, 53, Don Emmert, 33,
Focus On Sport, 26, Gary M. Prior, 46, 56, Greg Wood, 37, Jed Jacobsohn, 15, Jewel
Samad, 45, 59 (bottom), Ken Levine, 17, 31, Popperfoto, 19, Professional Sport,
42, Sean Garnsworthy, 57 (left), Stephane De Sakutin, 27, Stringer/Hulton Archive,
18, Tony Duffy, 25; Newscom: Abaca/Dubreuil Corinne, 41, 58, Atticus Images/Paul
Harris, 29, EPA/Andy Rain, 59 (top), Reuters/Gary Hershorn, 10, 11, Reuters/Kevin
Lamarque, 49, 57 (right), Reuters/Lucy Nicholson, 9, Reuters/Mike Blake, cover, 5, 6,
7, 13, 32, Reuters/Mike Segar, 35, SportsChrome/Sport the Library, 50, ZUMA Press/
Christopher Levy, 55; Shutterstock: Lev Radin, 48

Library of Congress Cataloging-in-Publication Data
Cataloging-in-publication information is on file with the Library of Congress.
ISBN 978-0-7565-5529-0 (library binding)
ISBN 978-0-7565-5533-7 (paperback)
ISBN 978-0-7565-5545-0 (ebook pdf)

Printed in the United States of America.
10018S17

TABLEOFCONTENTS

ChapterOne
HISTORIC MATCH

Evening fell in Flushing Meadows in Queens, in New York City, but the Arthur Ashe Stadium glowed bright as day under blazing lights. It was September 8, 2001, and more than 23,000 spectators packed seats surrounding the tennis court below. Enormous screens showed close-ups of the opening ceremony taking place.

Across the country, almost 23 million people watched on TV at home. For the first time ever, the U.S. Open women's singles finals match was being broadcast in prime time. It had not been squeezed between the men's semifinals matches in the afternoon, as usual. The finals match would be unlike any other in the past. "The Williams Sisters Have a Date With History," a *New York Times* headline that morning had announced. The sisters were the first to play each other in a major tournament in 117 years. And it was the first time both players in the Grand Slam finals were African-American.

Photojournalists gathered along the edges of the court, their cameras ready to record the historic match. On assignment for Reuters News Agency, Mike Blake trained his Canon DCS520 digital camera on the sisters. Twenty-one-year-old Venus Williams and her sister Serena, younger by 15 months, walked

The Williams sisters, Venus (left) and Serena, posed before the start of their historic match at the 2001 U.S. Open.

by in zipped warm-up jackets, holding flowers. They posed at the net with rackets, standing close to one another and smiling.

Blake's lens roamed the crowd and settled on Boris Becker of Germany, winner of the 1989 U.S. Open men's singles. Among the celebrities in the stands, Blake found and photographed filmmaker

Spike Lee, whose movies deal with challenges in the lives of African-Americans.

On the court below stood Diana Ross, a legendary African-American performer who herself had broken racial barriers. As she sang "God Bless America," the Harlem Gospel Choir swayed behind her in red and blue gowns. As the star of the musical trio The Supremes during the 1960s, a time of major racial unrest in the United States, Ross had been loved by both black and white audiences. Before leaving the court, Ross embraced a beaming Serena, who had made history just two years earlier. Just 17 years old then, she had won the U.S. Open women's singles championship, becoming the first black woman since 1958 to win a major tennis tournament. Making tennis history was a Williams family affair. In 2000 Venus became the first black woman in more than 40 years to win England's world-famous Wimbledon tournament.

Tennis officials delighted in the excitement over the Williams sisters' tennis match. "Night tennis, in New York, under the lights, with the world's top celebrity athletes, will provide a tremendous showcase," said Arlen Kantarian, the chief executive of the U.S. Tennis Association. In fact, the match drew 51 percent more TV viewers than the previous year.

Audiences expected a heroic battle for the trophy. They had already seen each Williams sister defeat her opponent in semifinals matches the day before. With powerful lenses, photojournalists had recorded

Legendary superstar Diana Ross

Serena's powerful play won out in her semifinal match against Martina Hingis.

close-up images of the action on the court. Blake had captured the yellow blur of the ball as Serena delivered powerful serves to Martina Hingis of Switzerland. Serena scored on every one of her 17 serves in the second set. Often Hingis could not even get her racket on the ball. Blake photographed

Hingis pressing her arm over her face in frustration. Praising Serena's power and strategy after the match, Hingis said, "She played smart. She waited for her chances. And she hit winners."

Blake's lens later found Serena in the audience, watching her sister's semifinals match. Again and again, Venus slung well-placed forehand shots and powerful backhands at Jennifer Capriati of the United States. Capriati was losing, and Blake photographed her during a break with a towel over her head, cradling her face. Later Capriati admitted that Venus had made her work so hard that she "ran out of gas."

Together the sisters had made history by reaching the finals as African-Americans. But facing each other across the net was a different challenge altogether. They had grown up training together and sharing the same bedroom. They had shared hotel rooms while traveling to competitions. They had even helped each other win games by pointing out the weaknesses of opponents. But now only one could have her named etched into the U.S. Open's silver trophy. Their mother, Oracene Price, watched from the player's box, wearing pins with each daughter's name. Unable to handle the stress, their father, Richard Williams, had flown home to Florida to avoid watching his daughters play each other.

Fireworks burst into the dark sky from the top of the roofless stadium. Venus in white and Serena in

ALWAYS CHANGING TECHNOLOGY

Reuters photographer Mike Blake (right) covered the 2016 election campaign.

News services are in the business of providing information to news organizations. More than a century ago, Reuters News Agency used telegraph cables and even carrier pigeons to send stories and photos to newspapers. Today images and stories travel wirelessly, but Mike Blake has seen technology change dramatically since beginning work at Reuters in 1985.

In the days of film cameras, Blake had to develop the film himself. He usually transformed a hotel bathroom into a makeshift darkroom. He then made an 8 x 10 print of each photo on special paper. "After drying the print with a hair dryer," he said, he would "wrap it on a drum transmitter called a 16S. The picture would spin around a drum and an electronic eye would scan across the image. We would have to take the mouthpiece off the hotel phone and clip two of the transmitter wires to the inside of the handset. The transmitter would convert the spinning image to sound and send it down the line to a picture desk who would then send it around the world."

In the late 1990s photojournalists started using digital cameras to gather images on computer chips. In 2001 they could take two images per second—today they can take up to 14. They can send images to editors even while an event is happening. Photo editors sort through hundreds or even thousands of images to select those that best capture an event. "Since moving to digital photography, the process is much quicker and simpler," Blake said. "I can transmit a picture wirelessly from my camera to our picture desk in Singapore, where they send it to our clients around the world instantly."

Yet despite the changes, a photojournalist's job remains a practical one. "The camera is really just like a hammer and nails," Blake said. "We use a camera to record what we see, just as a carpenter uses a hammer and nails to build a house. The technology has changed, we are able to record images with better quality and more speed than ever before, yet the essence of the still image has not changed. It's a moment frozen in time that will never happen again in any of our lives."

Venus stretched to return the ball to her sister.

yellow each took a side of the court. Microphones soon caught the sisters' grunts as they served balls at well over 100 mph (160 kph). Blake's lens caught their faces, tensed with the effort. They were well-matched, and viewers enjoyed their exciting volleys. In the second game of the match, the sisters tied four times and struggled for the winning point after reaching deuce.

Serena worked hard, but the accuracy of her match against Hingis was gone. She lashed out backhands and ground strokes that sometimes missed their mark or flew into the net. Blake captured her eyes clenched in frustration when Venus broke her serve in the first set. Serena's own mistakes also cost her many points.

By the end of the match, she had made 36 unforced errors, compared with Venus' 19.

Venus, meanwhile, played with the same calm power that defeated Capriati. Blake captured Venus mid-serve, her racket a vertical blur. She shot balls past her sister's racket. Her ball even knocked the racket out of Serena's hand in the fourth game of the match. Just 69 minutes after they had started, Venus easily won her second U.S. Open victory in a row (6-2, 6-4). But Venus did not throw up her arms joyfully, as she had when she defeated Capriati. The sisters met at the net and hugged. Venus whispered "I love you, all right?" to her younger sister.

Blake and other photographers hustled to get into position at the far end of the court for the trophy presentation. They took images from many angles of Venus and Serena posing with their trophies. Like the Williams sisters, the photographers also felt both camaraderie and competition on the court. "We are all very competitive," Blake said later, "and work hard at making the best possible images. Many of us compete with one another all day and night but also look out for each other and enjoy good, long-lasting friendships while living in all parts of the world."

After the match the sisters proved their smiles were genuine. "I'm disappointed," Serena said, "but only a little, because Venus won." Venus, the winner, explained that "I always want Serena to win. It's strange. I'm the bigger sister. I'm the one who takes care of her. I make sure she has everything even if I don't. I love her. It's hard."

"Venus is always the comforter," their mother said. She joked that "it doesn't matter who won the prize. Serena always spends Venus' money anyway." Photographs of the sisters holding the winner's and runner-up's trophies appeared in newspapers the next day. They showed two sisters who had battled each other on a tennis court. But they also captured two athletes who had fought, and would continue to fight, for a place for women and African-Americans in tennis and the world beyond.

Serena Williams (left) and big sister Venus proudly held their U.S. Open trophies.

ChapterTwo
BREAKING BARRIERS

A few months before the 2001 U.S. Open, the Williams sisters faced a stadium of hostile fans. The audience had been eagerly awaiting a semifinals match between Venus and Serena at a tournament in Indian Wells, California. But their enthusiasm turned to outrage when it was announced that Venus had withdrawn from the match because of a knee injury. A rumor circulated that the Williams family was avoiding a match between the sisters.

The Williams family would struggle for years to forget what happened. "All I could see," Serena said later, "was a sea of rich people—mostly older, mostly white—standing and booing like some kind of genteel lynch mob." Charles Pasarell, director of the tournament, later recalled "cringing when all that stuff was going on. It was unfair for the crowd to do that." Serena's father told reporters that the audience was saying, "Stay away from here, we don't want you here." Instead of Venus, Serena played fellow teenager Kim Clijsters and won the tournament.

But she and Venus refused to play at Indian Wells for years afterward. "It has been difficult for me to forget spending hours crying in the Indian Wells locker room after winning in 2001," Serena said, "driving back to Los Angeles feeling as if I had lost

The stadium was packed with outraged fans for Serena's match against Kim Clijsters. Neither Serena nor Venus would return to Indian Wells for many years.

the biggest game ever—not a mere tennis game but a bigger fight for equality."

For the Williams family, the experience at Indian Wells was a painful reminder of the country's history of unjust, and even brutal, treatment of black Americans. Enslaved Africans once worked on white-owned plantations in Louisiana, where Richard Williams grew up. Even after slavery ended, following the Civil War, African-Americans did not enjoy basic freedoms. Laws in many parts of the United States required blacks and whites to live separate lives. They could not attend the same schools. They could not marry each other. In 1892 an African-American named Homer Plessy was jailed for boarding a whites-only train in New Orleans. This event in Richard's home state resulted in a Supreme Court decision that only strengthened the U.S. government's determination to enforce segregation.

Richard grew up in the city of Shreveport during the 1940s and 1950s. He saw firsthand that black Americans did not have the same rights as whites. When a white driver ran over and killed an African-American man, Williams recalled that the driver blamed the victim and "there was no investigation, there was no police car." What's more, his hometown was the headquarters of Louisiana's Ku Klux Klan. The racist group harassed, beat, and even murdered African-Americans in southern states.

Williams and his wife, Oracene Price, chose to raise their daughters in Los Angeles County, California, an area that also was shaped by nearly a century of racial tension. The population surged in the 1940s, when millions of African-Americans moved there in search of a better life. But not all white residents were welcoming. In fact, Compton, where the Williams family lived, banned African-Americans until after World War II.

Venus Williams learned to play tennis in the tough California city of Compton, south of downtown Los Angeles.

Compton later became the first city in the West to have a government made up entirely of African-Americans. But gangs of whites patrolled the city to intimidate black residents and keep their neighborhoods—however overcrowded—from spilling into white areas.

During the civil rights era of the 1960s, federal legislation finally allowed African-Americans to demand access to better housing, schools, and jobs. They demanded an end to harsh treatment by white police. But lingering frustrations sparked protests and civil unrest. When Venus and Serena were growing up in the 1980s, unemployment, poverty, and violent

Only men could play tennis at Wimbledon in its early days.

crime were part of daily life. Members of gangs such as the Crips and the Bloods used guns to control neighborhoods and to sell drugs illegally.

The Williams sisters grew up far from the birthplace of their beloved sport. Kings and monks in Europe played an indoor game similar to tennis for centuries. In the late 1800s, an Englishman adapted the game so it could be played outdoors on lawns. Elegantly dressed Victorian men and women enjoyed this "lawn tennis" at garden parties. Soon players became more competitive. The first tournament for men was played in 1877 at Wimbledon, which is near London, England. At first the organizers refused to

Maud Watson won the first women's final at Wimbledon in 1884.

allow women to compete, but finally, in 1884, the first Wimbledon women's event took place. Two sisters, Maud and Lilian Watson, met in the finals. They played in stiff corsets, petticoats, and long sleeves and skirts, but their white clothing helped to disguise their perspiration. Maud defeated her older sister to win a silver flower basket and become Wimbledon's first women's champion.

By the 1870s the game had made its way across the Atlantic Ocean to U.S. sports clubs. Americans formed the United States Lawn Tennis Association (USLTA) in 1881. Their players competed in international tennis tournaments beginning in 1900, when they played Great Britain for the Davis Cup.

But tennis courts in the United States provided no shelter from racism. Private clubs had tennis courts, but most of them denied membership to non-white players even into the late 1900s. When the USLTA made a rule that African-American players were not allowed in its tournaments, more than a dozen tennis clubs made up of black players took quick action.

They formed the American Tennis Association (ATA) in 1916. The organization held its own competitions for African-American players on the courts of black colleges such as Morehouse College in Atlanta, Georgia. For decades USLTA players refused to compete against ATA players. In the 1920s USLTA star Helen Wills Moody refused to play Ora Washington, who became an undefeated ATA champion for 12 years.

It took great courage to break down the wall between the ATA and the USLTA. African-American tennis player Althea Gibson boldly applied to play in the 1950 U.S. National Championships (now the U.S.

Private clubs had tennis courts, but most of them denied membership to non-white players even into the late 1900s.

New York City's Cosmopolitan Tennis Club in Harlem was affiliated with the ATA. Some of the players posed by the net when the club hosted the New York State Negro Tennis Championships in 1940.

Open) in Forest Hills, New York. A four-time winner of the whites-only tournament, Alice Marble, supported her bid. Marble criticized the USLTA's ban on black players in an article in *American Lawn Tennis* magazine. "If Althea Gibson represents a challenge to the present crop of players," she wrote, "then it's only fair that they meet this challenge on the courts."

USLTA leaders gave in, and Gibson, who was 23, became the first African-American player to compete in a major tennis tournament. She did not stop there. She won the French championship in 1956, becoming the first person of color to win a Grand Slam event. In 1957 she was Wimbledon's first black player when Queen Elizabeth II presented her with the winner's trophy. Gibson returned to Forest Hills in 1957 to complete the work she had started seven years earlier: She became the first black player to win the U.S. Nationals. Vice President Richard Nixon

presented her with the trophy, which was filled with flowers. Audiences in 1958 marveled as Gibson added a second Wimbledon trophy and a second U.S. Nationals trophy to her collection.

Despite being a champion, Gibson, like other African-Americans, faced discrimination in her daily life. She was a tennis champion, yet hotels refused to rent her rooms. She wrote in her autobiography that "Shaking hands with the Queen of England was a long way from being forced to sit in the colored section of the bus going into downtown Wilmington,

OPENING DOORS

Althea Gibson, on her way to becoming Wimbledon's first African-American singles champion

Lightning knocked an eagle sculpture off the top of the stadium during a match Althea Gibson was playing in the 1950 U.S. National Championships. "When lightning put down that eagle," she said, "maybe it was an omen that times was changing." Gibson didn't win the 1950 tournament, now called the U.S. Open, but she was on her way to throwing open doors of opportunity for black tennis players all over the world.

Gibson was born in 1927 to poor farmers in South Carolina. The family moved to New York City's Harlem neighborhood three years later in search of a better life. Her championship talent in table tennis led her to tennis and further success. She won her first junior tennis championship in 1944.

But life as tennis champion was not always rewarding. She could not earn enough by playing to support herself. She also faced racial slurs on and off the court from the time she started playing tennis. Yet she was also admired. After winning the Wimbledon singles title in 1957, an estimated 100,000 people attended a parade in her honor in New York City. She was the first black woman on the covers of *Sports Illustrated* and *Time* magazines. And Arthur Ashe Stadium, named after the tennis pioneer and home to the U.S. Open, was dedicated on her 70th birthday in 1997.

North Carolina." Tennis players today speak of Gibson's accomplishments with gratitude. "If it hadn't been for her," Billie Jean King, the winner of 12 Grand Slam titles, has said, "it wouldn't have been so

Arthur Ashe proved to be a winner on and off the court.

easy for Arthur [Ashe] or the ones who followed."

Arthur Ashe used his tennis racket to help change a world plagued by racism. When Serena walks into Arthur Ashe Stadium to play, she remembers the history of the place "named after someone who's broken so many barriers."

When he was growing up in the 1950s, Ashe wrote, "white people in Virginia told me what I could do, where I could go to church, in which taxi I could ride, where I had to sit on the bus, in which stores I could try on a coat." He has said that despite facing terrible health problems, "being black is the greatest burden I've had to bear." But he decided that "racism is not an excuse to not do the best you can." He learned to play tennis on the courts in the segregated city parks of Richmond, Virginia. Coaches in an ATA program for talented African-American players noticed him. Besides seeing his talent, they thought his calm personality—later described as an "icy elegance"—would help him handle the discrimination he would face as a black tennis player.

Ashe made tennis history in 1968, the year when the assassination of civil rights leader Martin Luther King Jr. sparked riots and turmoil around the country. In the U.S. Open men's singles competition, Ashe hit an astonishing 26 aces to defeat top-ranked Dutch player Tom Okker. He was the first African-American to win a men's singles title in any Grand Slam tournament. Ashe repeated the accomplishment at the Australian Open in 1970 and at Wimbledon in 1975, when he defeated U.S. champion Jimmy Connors.

But Ashe wanted more than trophies and fame. He wanted to use tennis to improve the lives of black people around the world. He made a historic trip to Johannesburg, South Africa, in 1973 to be the first black player in the South African Open. He hoped to inspire black South Africans who were struggling with apartheid, a system that forced blacks to live separately from whites. He hosted a tennis clinic in Soweto, a black community of 1 million people living in poverty outside the capital. Ashe never forgot a

Arthur Ashe lifted the singles trophy at the 1975 Wimbledon tennis tournament.

Serena Williams and her sister worked with young players at a tennis clinic at the Arthur Ashe Academy in Soweto, South Africa.

young black South African who told him he was the first free black man he had ever seen.

Today Serena Williams praises those who opened doors for her, her sister, and all athletes and other people of color. A memory of Ashe teaching her and her sister as children at a tennis clinic still inspires her. "Because of what he went through, because of what he did, I have an opportunity to play," she said. "I have an opportunity to be the best that I can be because of him."

ChapterThree
AMAZING SUCCESS

The Williams sisters knew expectations were high for their U.S. Open finals match in 2001. Venus had predicted an exciting match. "A lot of matches we have played haven't been considered championship, heroic matches," she said. "I think this will be different." But critics were unimpressed. Looking back, sports journalist Peter Bodo even called it a "pretty lousy match." But Mike Blake's image of the smiling African-American sisters holding trophies is part of a larger story that is dramatic and full of surprises.

The Williams sisters' story began with a bold plan in 1980. After watching Romania's Virginia Ruzici receive a check on TV for winning a tennis tournament, Richard Williams declared to his wife, Oracene, that "we have two kids, and we'll become rich. They're going to be tennis players." He wrote a 78-page plan outlining how his daughters would reach the top of the tennis world. Using books and instructional videos, Williams taught himself and his wife the basics of the game. Together they began teaching their five children, Venus and Serena and their three older half-sisters.

While other tennis players were training with professional coaches in private sports clubs and

Venus (left) and Serena with their father, Richard Williams, at the Compton tennis courts in 1991

sports centers, the Williams sisters followed a different path. Their parents coached them on gritty public courts in Compton. They had to drop to the ground when gunfire volleyed between gang members. "Belief and training" was the formula for the sisters' success, according to Venus. Beyond teaching tennis skills, their parents worked to prepare the sisters for situations like the one they faced at Indian Wells. It was a place, Richard Williams pointed out, where "the whole crowd turned against

[Serena] and all she had to do was remember the training that she had been through." Raising his daughters in the crime-filled city of Compton in the early 1980s was part of his plan to raise successful athletes. "There was no place in the world that was rougher than Compton," he said. "The ghetto will make you rough, it'll make you tough, it'll make you strong." But gang-related violence would also bring tragedy. Venus and Serena lost an older half-sister, Yetunde, in 2003 in a drive-by shooting in Compton.

Proof of the effectiveness of their parents' unconventional coaching came early. "Venus and Serena took to tennis as soon as rackets were put in their hands," said an older half-sister, Lyndrea. By 1991 both girls were top-ranked in their local tennis divisions, Venus in the 12-and-under and Serena in the 10-and-under. Ten years later at the U.S. Open finals, their mother said, "I'm not really surprised. This is what was expected of them. I never allowed words like 'can't' and 'pressure' into their vocabulary. I knew they would get to this place." Although Williams and Price had exposed their daughters to the harsh realities of Compton, they also sheltered them by moving to Florida in 1991. There the girls avoided junior tournaments to conserve energy and prepare for tennis careers with a professional tennis coach.

"Venus and Serena took to tennis as soon as rackets were put in their hands."

Venus (left) and Serena worked on their game at a Florida tennis academy in 1992.

Before photographing the Williams sisters, Mike Blake also followed a direct path to his profession. "I knew right out of high school that I wanted to record the world around me with a camera," he said. Snapping photographs of skateboarders

Mike Blake's camera caught hockey great Wayne Gretzky screaming with joy after the Edmonton Oilers won the Stanley Cup for the fourth time in 1988.

in his hometown of Toronto, Canada, led him to photojournalism and the chance to take his camera close to the action of many sports. "The more effort you put into something, the more reward you will get at the end of it," Blake said. "I have been lucky enough in my career to have covered major events all around the world for Reuters. From Wayne Gretzky lifting up a Stanley Cup, Michael Jordan sinking a

Venus, at 17, made it to the finals of the U.S. Open.

game-winning shot to win the NBA Championships and Tiger Woods winning a Masters. ... [It's] sometimes fun to look back at the pictures because they end up being a big part of your life's story."

Blake's lens was waiting when 17-year-old Venus stepped into the international spotlight at the U.S. Open in 1997. It was the first time she had made it to the finals of a Grand Slam event. But the situation looked bleak—Venus was a 66th-ranked player while her opponent, 16-year-old Martina Hingis, was the number one female player in the world.

Photographers' cameras captured Venus' courageous battle. Hundreds of red, white, and blue beads woven into her braids rattled together as she pounded the ball with a shout. During short breaks, she studied handwritten notes reminding her to concentrate and to keep her form. Blake's photographs from the match show Hingis kissing the trophy after winning 6-0, 6-4. Venus, meanwhile, had to settle for the runner-up trophy. But the newcomer had already caught the world's attention as the first African-American woman to reach the U.S. Open finals since Althea Gibson did 39 years earlier.

Earlier in 1997 Blake had photographed a 21-year-old Tiger Woods breaking down color barriers in golf—a sport Gibson had also tackled. She was the first black woman to play on a professional golf tour. Blake's photographs captured Woods putting on the green jacket reserved for winners of the Masters —the first African-American to do so. But Woods' smile hid the struggle that many minority athletes have faced in golf, as in tennis. Not until 1975 were black players allowed to compete in the tournament in Augusta, Georgia. They weren't allowed to be members of the club there until 1990.

At the 1999 U.S. Open, Serena joined her sister in changing the image of the professional tennis player. This time Venus lost in the semifinals. She watched the finals match from the stands as 17-year-old Serena stood in the same place Venus had in 1997— facing Hingis, now 18 years old. It was Serena's first time in the finals of a major tournament, yet she quickly unnerved her seasoned opponent and

Singles runner-up Martina Hingis and winner Serena Williams at the 1999 U.S. Open

dominated the first set. Hingis later admitted she felt she was losing during most of the match. In the last game, the panting players slammed balls at each other with the score tied again and again. Then Hingis' backhand shot missed its mark and Serena won, 6-3, 7-6. The younger Williams became the first African-American woman to win a major title since Gibson. Hingis herself praised the display of skill in Serena's game, adding "I don't think it can get much better."

Price believes tough competition has also driven her daughters to be champions. After Serena's historic win in 1999, Price said, "That day meant Venus had to stop playing around and get serious. It was a wake-up call for Venus." Perhaps as a result, Venus battled her way to the finals of the 2000 U.S. Open. But she was hardly the inexperienced teenager of 1997—she was now a world champion with a silver trophy for winning the singles title at Wimbledon. She would also win singles gold at the 2000 Olympics in Australia.

To reach the 2000 U.S. Open finals, Venus had defeated Hingis in a hard-fought semifinals match. Venus then faced U.S. player Lindsay Davenport, who earlier had beaten Serena in the quarterfinals. Davenport started out strong and took the lead. Then Venus adjusted her strategy, switching from playing with full power to focusing on patience and endurance. Venus went on to win the match (6-4, 7-5) and her first U.S. Open trophy.

The next year's U.S. Open finals match was memorable, but not for great performances by the two sisters, who were playing against each other. Critics pointed out that Serena lost control of her game and that Venus seemed to simply wait for her sister to make mistakes. The sisters have admitted that shifting between being sisters and playing as opponents can be tricky. "Right now we're competitors," Serena said in 2009, "and then

Venus (left) raised the arm of her younger sister Serena after beating her in straight sets at the 1998 Australian Open.

the moment we shake hands and we're done with this match, we're sisters. But I'm always happy for Venus, and she's even more happy for me." They first met as opponents in a Grand Slam event at the 1998 Australian Open. "Today would have been great fun if it were a final," Venus said, "but it wasn't so fun to eliminate my little sister in the second round." Venus didn't make it to the women's singles finals but did win her first Grand Slam title as part of a mixed doubles team.

On September 8, 2001, photojournalists captured an important twist in the Williams sisters' story. In Blake's photograph, Venus holds the U.S. Open trophy. But next to her, the runner-up is poised to begin a rapid climb to join the world's greatest tennis players. Legendary player Chris Evert would later call Serena "a phenomenon that once every hundred years comes around." World-famous champion John McEnroe called her "the greatest player, I think, that ever lived."

Both sisters reached the top of the tennis world in 2002. For three weeks, Venus was the top-ranked female tennis player in the world, the first black player to achieve this since Arthur Ashe held the men's top ranking in 1975. But then the sisters' story shifts focus. The sisters played each other in the finals of the French Open that April. Serena held the winner's trophy as Venus, the runner-up, grabbed a camera to take photographs. Three months later they met again in the Wimbledon finals.

After defeating her sister again, Serena explained that "at the beginning of the year, I told myself I don't care what else happens this year, I want to win Wimbledon." And she did. Now Serena reached the number one ranking in the world, a position she held for 57 weeks. Serena credits the natural competition between sisters for driving her to success. "Being kind of the little sister and the one that wasn't as strong and wasn't as good yet gave me

Billie Jean King and Bobby Riggs shook hands after King trounced Riggs in their Battle of the Sexes in 1973.

MOVING FORWARD

Many assumed it would be an easy victory for the former top-ranked men's tennis player Bobby Riggs when he challenged Billie Jean King, the top women's player, to a tennis match. Boy, were they wrong. King easily defeated Riggs in the 1973 "Battle of the Sexes" at the Houston Astrodome. It was one of many steps toward equality in tennis.

After the match, *The New York Times* reported that King had "struck a proud blow for herself and women around the world with a crushing 6-4, 6-3, 6-3 rout of Bobby Riggs" in the $100,000 winner-take-all match. The newspaper said King's win "ended the bizarre saga" of Riggs, "the 55-year-old hustler, who had bolted to national prominence with his blunt putdowns of women's tennis and the role of today's female."

Earlier the same year King had founded the Women's Tennis Association, which is the official organizing group for women's professional tennis. Among other goals, it has worked to gain equal prize money for female tennis players. At the time of its founding, prizes for male players were more than 10 times those for female players. The U.S. Open offered equal prize money in 1973, but not until 2007 did the four major Grand Slam tournaments all offer equal prize money.

encouragement, and gave me the fight that I have in my game," she said.

Spectators packed the stands of Arthur Ashe Stadium in record numbers for the 2002 U.S. Open women's final. They stood and clapped for the Williams sisters, who were about to face off in yet another final. Aretha Franklin sang the national anthem before the champions hugged at the net. This time the younger sister dominated the older one. "When I'm playing her," Serena has said, "I don't think of her as my sister. When you're in the moment you don't really think about it. We trained all our lives to play on this court and on this stage. ... It's a great honor." Serena made powerful, controlled shots in long volleys with Venus. She pumped her fist after scoring points. She pointed with her racket at balls that landed out of bounds to make sure the judges had not missed Venus' miscalculation. Venus delivered precise backhands with a serious face. But as pressure mounted, she began to lose control of her serve. Serena won, 6-4, 6-3.

A few months later Serena defeated Venus again, this time in 105 Fahrenheit (41 Celsius) degree heat at the Australian Open. She joined the ranks of tennis greats Martina Navratilova and Steffi Graf as winners of four Grand Slam titles in a row. Venus did not beat her sister again in the finals of a Grand Slam event until 2008, when they met on the grass court at

Venus was all smiles after winning the Wimbledon singles trophy in 2008.

Wimbledon. Serena took charge of the game early, but her accuracy wavered under Venus' high-speed serves. The older sister won the Wimbledon trophy for the fifth time. But the following year, they met again on the grass, and Serena defeated her sister with 12 aces, winning every set she served.

The sisters have played against each other in Grand Slam tournaments 14 times. But they have also played many times on the same side of the net. Their close relationship, paired with their talent, has made them a formidable doubles team. They took the world by storm in doubles play beginning in 1999. They held up twin trophies at the French Open. And after Serena's historic U.S. Open singles win, she and Venus made history the next day. They won the doubles events to become the first black women's team to ever win the tournament. Cameras caught smiling sisters posing with the silver bowl, their pet Yorkshire terriers peeking over the rim. By 2016, the sisters had won a record 14 Grand Slam doubles titles.

Venus and Serena did more than score points as a doubles team. They scored points for their country, and made history again doing it. U.S. player Zina Garrison had already become the first black tennis player to win Olympic gold. She won a gold medal in doubles and a bronze medal in singles at the 1988 Olympics in Seoul, South Korea. The Williams sisters won doubles gold in Sydney, Australia, by defeating

Venus (left) and Serena smiled and held hands after winning doubles gold at the Beijing Olympics.

the team from the Netherlands in 2000. Photographs show the first sisters to win Olympic gold in doubles in red, white, and blue warm-up suits, side by side, raising their gold medals high. They won doubles gold again at the 2008 Beijing Olympics and at the 2012 London Games. They were upset in the first round of the 2016 Olympics in Rio de Janeiro, falling to a team from the Czech Republic.

Mike Blake and other photographers were courtside when Serena won her first gold medal in

"There's something about standing next to Venus and holding that gold medal."

singles at the 2012 London Olympics. His high-speed camera captured Serena after her victory, in midair with arms outstretched, her red, white, and blue skirt billowing. When she and her sister won gold in doubles again, they slapped high-fives after the victory. They are the first doubles team ever to win three gold medals. "There's something about standing next to Venus and holding that gold medal," Serena said. Only three female tennis players have won two gold medals at the same Olympics—Serena in 2012, Venus in 2000, and Helen Wills Moody in 1924, the player who had refused to play African-American star Ora Washington decades earlier.

Today the sisters have made peace with playing each other. Venus' agent Carlos Fleming said, "In the early days, they would play each other in a final and go back to a hotel suite they shared, and there would be flowers waiting for the winner. Imagine what that was like." Fleming marveled that Venus accepts having "a member of her family exceed her in the way Serena has, and the relationship stayed intact, actually strengthened."

Today the sisters even seem inspired by the chance to play each other. Before meeting in the 2015 U.S. Open quarterfinals, Serena said, "I think it's more fun than it used to be. We really relish the opportunity. We're happy to still be involved in getting so far, and it's still super intense."

ChapterFour
HELPING OTHERS

Cameras captured the sisters together again in December 2015. They weren't under stadium lights, but stage lights in New York City. They stood in fashionable gowns, their hair loose rather than pulled back under visors and sweatbands. Venus wiped away tears as she introduced Serena as *Sports Illustrated*'s Sportsperson of the Year. "It's been an honor to be your big sister," she said. "It's the best job in the world. I love you so much." The honoree was 34 years old, an age when many athletes are considering retirement, and for the second time she had won four major titles in a row, a so-called Serena Slam. Her Grand Slam singles titles totaled a near-record-breaking 21. Again, she had reached and maintained a three-year hold on the number-one world ranking.

Venus told the audience that her sister's triumphs were about more than tennis. "Living her dream was more than living her own dream," Venus said. "She was living the world's dream." Serena was the first woman in more than 30 years to be honored individually by *Sports Illustrated*. And she was the first black woman ever to receive the sportsperson award individually.

As far back as 2001, Oracene Price had predicted that her daughters would have an impact on the world.

Oracene Price beamed with pride as daughter Venus (right) presented the Sportsperson of the Year award to daughter Serena in 2015.

"I don't think they can even appreciate what this means right now," she said before their U.S. Open finals match. "It's the real deal, though. It's like no one knew the impact Ali made until it registered in the history books."

Photojournalists, like professional athletes, "don't really think about the history at the time, you're too busy doing your job," according to Mike Blake. Yet the images captured by Blake and other photojournalists at the 2001 trophy presentation were

Serena (left) and Venus were popular among their fellow athletes at the 2000 Sydney Games, where they won doubles gold.

not just of prize-winning athletes. They showed the rise of women of color in a sport that has neglected female players and disrespected black players for decades. Today's sports figures appreciate the extraordinary success of the sisters. Mary Carillo, a sportscaster and former tennis player, noticed athletes snapping pictures of the young sisters at the 2000 Summer Olympics. She said she was "thrilled that it was two women's tennis players all these Olympians wanted to pose with."

The Williams sisters have helped pull women's tennis into the spotlight. Their 2001 prime-time televised match was a "significant breakthrough for the coverage of tennis on television," said USTA chief executive Arlen Kantarian. Attracting viewers to tennis has been a struggle since its wide popularity in the 1970s. But interest in women's tennis is on the rise. When Serena played in the 2015 U.S. Open, the event for the first time sold out before the men's final did.

Female players' struggle for respect is far from over, though. In March 2016, before a finals match between Serena Williams and Victoria Azarenka of Belarus, BNP Paribas tournament director Raymond Moore said men's tennis has "carried the sport." He said the Women's Tennis Association rides "on the coattails of the men." His words outraged many around the world, including Serena. She said his words were a "disservice" to Billie Jean King and "every woman on this planet that has ever tried to stand up for what they believed in and being proud to be a woman." Moore resigned his position.

Photographs of Serena have shown the world that she also battles old-fashioned ideas in another way— simply in the way she dresses for competition. Instead of traditional white clothing, Serena said, she tries to "bring pop culture to tennis" with leopard prints,

Serena's outfits showcase vivid colors and prints on the court.

moon boots, body suits, and outfits of many colors. Her fashion choices, she said, remind women that "you can be beautiful and powerful at the same time."

The sisters also broke stereotypes by showing women that they can play as hard and fast as men. Until it was broken in 2014 by Sabine Lisicki's 131-mph (211-kph) serve, Venus held the women's record for fastest serve for seven years. Serena's control of her power is widely admired. Sports columnist Christopher Clarey wrote that Serena's "power serving and her serving under pressure are weapons that no other great player has possessed

USTA TODAY

Venus (left) and Serena are credited with bringing many African-Americans to competitive tennis..

The U.S. Tennis Association has come a long way from the days when it had rules to keep out black players. In 2015 Katrina Adams became the first African-American and first former professional player to take over leadership of the sport's national governing body. As a child, she saw Arthur Ashe playing at Wimbledon on television in 1975 and announced, "I'm going there one day." She later made it to the final rounds of Wimbledon, and she won 20 Women's Tennis Association doubles titles. She believes that Venus and Serena are responsible for the many African-Americans playing and competing today. She said, "It goes to show you that if there's someone out there that looks like you that you can see and hear, it kind of motivates you."

Today USTA wants to see results. "We want to make tennis look like America when it comes to cultural backgrounds," Adams said. Part of its mission now is attracting more minority players and coaches to the sport. After-school programs with support from USTA focus not only on bringing tennis to urban communities, but also on promoting something that helped the Williams sisters succeed: what a former participant called a "sense of family."

The Williams sisters brought power and agile play to the finals of the 2003 Australian Open.

to the same degree." Australian tennis player Samantha Stosur has said, "She is a great athlete, man or woman. There are a lot of guys who would love to do what she's been able to do, especially on a tennis court."

But some observers have found fault with so much physical power in women's tennis. They have even considered it to be unnatural. Althea Gibson had a chromosome test to prove to doubters that she was not a man in disguise. Some people have argued that the Williams sisters' playing style relies on power and very little strategy. Yet others praise their "feathery touch shots and clever angles." The combination of power and strategy is the reason for their success, said sports broadcaster Mary Carillo. Venus and Serena are "remarkable defensive players," she said. "They kept alive balls that no woman had ever kept in play." Serena said that playing is a "lot more than just hitting the ball as hard as you can. It's all about strategy and moving your opponent and just really figuring them out."

The Williams sisters have fought other battles—off the court. "I've had people look down on me, put me down because I didn't look like them—I look stronger, I've had people look past me because [of] the color of my skin, I've had people overlook me because I was a woman," Serena told the crowd when accepting *Sports Illustrated*'s 2015 Sportsperson of the Year award. She wrote then that "I'm a black woman, and I am in a sport that wasn't really meant for black people."

Some argue that sponsors also have not treated Serena fairly. Companies pay sports celebrities millions of dollars to help sell their products by wearing them and appearing in advertisements. The Russian player Maria Sharapova earned $10 million more in endorsements in 2015 than Serena did, even though Serena has dominated their tennis matches for years. Serena shrugged it off and said, "If they want to market someone who is white and blond, that's their choice." She added, "I have a lot of [business] partners who are very happy to work with me."

The Williams sisters' confidence in the face of challenges applies beyond tennis. "My Mom wanted all us girls to be strong black women," Serena said. When they were young, their father would put up homemade signs in their front yard with messages such as "Venus, You Must Take Control of Your Future." Their parents used creativity and discipline to overcome limited opportunities. Following in their footsteps, the sisters have continued the tradition of helping young people of color to succeed.

Althea Gibson believed that "no matter what accomplishments you make, somebody helped you." ATA Champion Ora Washington gave free coaching to young people at the public tennis courts in Germantown, Pennsylvania, where she got her own start in tennis. Arthur Ashe helped young people in 500 U.S. cities by co-founding a tennis program now managed by the USTA (formerly the USLTA.) He helped train Yannick Noah, a player in Cameroon, who also became a world-famous player. Noah won the French Open in 1983, making him and Ashe the only two black men to win Grand Slam men's singles titles.

As a child, Serena hit balls with Zina Garrison at a youth clinic. Garrison had made history at Wimbledon in 1990 as the first African-American woman since Althea Gibson to reach the finals of a Grand Slam tournament. Three years later she used

"My Mom wanted all us girls to be strong black women."

History-making Zina Garrison at Wimbledon in 1990

tennis tournament prize money to open a tennis academy in Houston, Texas, to help support inner-city youth through tennis and education.

Today the Williams sisters work to continue the cycle. "Zina Garrison, Althea Gibson, Arthur Ashe and Venus opened so many doors for me. I'm just opening the next door for the next person," Serena said. The sisters founded the Venus and Serena Williams Tutorial/Tennis Academy to help inner-city high school students in Los Angeles use tennis to prepare them for the future. Students train on the court, but they also work with tutors on academic subjects to help them get to college, ideally with scholarships. The Williams sisters embrace being role models. "I play for me," said Serena, "but I also play [for] and represent something much greater than me." Their millions of followers on social media prove that their reach has been global. Serena's coach, Patrick Mouratoglou, said the sisters "made people know that anyone that comes from anywhere, rich or not, can play and be successful."

But while traveling the world playing as a tennis icon, Serena Williams avoided one tournament in the California desert—until 2015. That year she returned to play at Indian Wells for the first time in 14 years. Her explanation was simple: "I'm just following my heart on this one."

When she walked into the stadium, the audience stood and clapped for a full minute. An African-American girl held up a sign that read "Straight Outta Compton." Serena fought tears, placing her hand over her heart. Later in the week she was forced to withdraw from the tournament semifinals because of injury, but the crowd was supportive this time. And before she addressed them,

The Williams sisters were warmly welcomed when they returned to Indian Wells.

the stadium announcer put his arm around Serena and said, "Welcome home. You belong here, we love you, and welcome back to Indian Wells." Venus followed her sister's lead and returned to Indian Wells in 2016. She, too, received a warm welcome. The sisters were indeed back—and looking to the future.

Timeline

1980

Venus Williams is born June 17 in Lynwood, California

1981

Serena Williams is born September 26 in Saginaw, Michigan

1991

The Williams family moves from California to Florida so Venus and Serena can train with tennis coach Rick Macci

2000

Venus wins Wimbledon and the U.S. Open; she and Serena win the Wimbledon doubles title; Venus wins singles gold at the Sydney Olympics; she and Serena win doubles gold

2001

Venus defeats Serena to win the U.S. Open; the sisters win the Australian Open doubles title

1997

Venus makes it to the U.S. Open finals at age 17

1999

Serena wins the U.S. Open at age 17; she and Venus win doubles titles at the French Open and U.S. Open

2002

Venus and Serena win the Wimbledon doubles title; they both reach number one world ranking during the year; Serena defeats Venus in four straight Grand Slam events—the French Open, Wimbledon, and the U.S. Open, and, in 2003, the Australian Open—for a Serena Slam

2003

Serena defeats Venus to win Wimbledon; the sisters win the Australian Open doubles title

2005 and 2007

Serena wins the Australian Open both years; Venus wins Wimbledon both years

Timeline

2009

Serena wins the Australian Open and defeats Venus to win Wimbledon; Venus and Serena win doubles titles at the Australian Open, Wimbledon, and the U.S. Open

2008

Venus defeats Serena to win Wimbledon; the sisters win the Wimbledon doubles title and doubles gold at the Beijing Olympics; Serena wins the U.S. Open

2013

Serena wins the French Open and the U.S. Open

2014

Serena wins the U.S. Open

2010

Serena wins the Australian Open and Wimbledon; the sisters win doubles titles at the Australian Open and the French Open

2012

Serena wins Wimbledon and the U.S. Open; Serena wins gold at the London Olympics; Venus and Serena win the doubles title at Wimbledon and doubles gold at the Olympics

2015

Serena wins the Australian Open, the French Open, and Wimbledon, which, combined with 2014's U.S. Open win, gives her a second Serena Slam; she is named *Sports Illustrated*'s Sportsperson of the Year

2016

Serena, who has been ranked number one since 2013, wins Wimbledon for the seventh time, and with Venus wins the Wimbledon doubles title; Serena's 22 Grand Slam singles titles tie her with Steffi Graf for the most wins in major tournaments; Serena becomes the world's highest-paid female athlete

Glossary

ace—point scored in tennis when a player serves and the opponent does not touch the ball

apartheid—former policy of racial segregation and discrimination in South Africa

barrier—something that blocks the way

break—when the server loses the game

civil rights—rights that all Americans have, including the right to equal treatment, under the law

clinic—short course on a subject or skill

deuce—tie score of 40-all in a tennis game requiring one player to get two consecutive points to win

discrimination—unfair treatment of people, often because of race, religion, gender, sexual preference, or age

Grand Slam—any of the four most important tennis tournaments—the Australian Open, the French Open, Wimbledon, and the U.S. Open; also called majors

minority—group of people different from a larger group of which it is a part because of race, religion, politics, or nationality

segregation—practice of separating people of different races, income classes, or ethnic groups

serve—overhead shot to put a ball into play

stereotype—widely held but oversimplified idea of a person or thing

unforced error—missed shot or lost point that is the result of the player's own mistake

Additional Resources

Further Reading

Anniss, Matt. *Venus & Serena Williams in the Community.*
New York : Britannica Educational Publishing / Rosen
Publishing Group, 2014

Schatz, Kate. *Rad American Women A-Z.*
San Francisco: City Lights Books, 2015

Zuckerman, Gregory, with Elijah and Gabriel Zuckerman.
*Rising Above: How 11 Athletes Overcame Challenges in
Their Youth to Become Stars.*
New York: Philomel Books, 2016.

Internet Sites

Use FactHound to find Internet sites related
to this book. All of the sites on FactHound
have been researched by our staff.

Here's all you do:
Visit *www.facthound.com*
Type in this code: 9780756555290

Critical Thinking Using the Common Core

Using examples from the text, explain how African-American tennis players have been treated unjustly in the past century. In what ways have black players overcome the challenges? (Key Ideas and Details)

In what ways have being sisters helped push Venus and Serena Williams into becoming exceptional tennis players and champions? (Integration of Knowledge and Ideas)

Discuss the ways in which the attitudes and actions of the Williams sisters reflect the influence of legendary black tennis players who came before them. (Integration of Knowledge and Ideas)

Source Notes

Page 4, line 14: Selena Roberts. "Tennis; The Williams Sisters Have a Date With History." *The New York Times*. 8 Sept. 2001. 17 Oct. 2016. http://www.nytimes.com/2001/09/08/sports/tennis-the-williams-sisters-have-a-date-with-history.html

Page 6, line 20: "Women To Serve Up Prime-time Final." *Chicago Tribune*. 21 March 2001. 17 Oct. 2016. http://articles.chicagotribune.com/2001-03-21/sports/0103210092_1_tennis-association-sanex-wta-tour-ericsson

Page 8, line 3: "Tennis; The Williams Sisters Have a Date With History."

Page 8, line 12: Ibid.

Page 9, col. 1, line 11: Mike Blake. Email interview. 11 March 2016.

Page 9, col. 2, line 6: Ibid.

Page 9, col. 2, line 12: Ibid.

Page 11, line 13: Jane McManus. "Venus stops Serena for U.S. Open title." *The* (Westchester, N.Y.) *Journal News*. 9 Sept. 2001. 17 Oct. 2016. http://usatoday30.usatoday.com/sports/tennis/01open/stories/2001-09-08-women-game.htm

Page 12, line 6: Mike Blake.

Page 12, line 13: Mike Puma. "Venus defeats Serena in 2001 U.S. Open final." ESPN Classic. 8 Sept. 2004. 17 Oct. 2016. http://espn.go.com/classic/s/add_williams_venus_and_serena.html

Page 12, line 15: Selena Roberts. "Tennis; The Night Belongs to Venus." *The New York Times*. 9 Sept. 2001. 17 Oct. 2016. http://www.nytimes.com/2001/09/09/sports/tennis-the-night-belongs-to-venus.html?pagewanted=all

Page 12, line 19: Ibid

Page 14, line 11: Kerry Howley. "The Unretiring Serena Williams." *New York Magazine*. 9 Aug. 2015. 17 Oct. 2016. http://nymag.com/thecut/2015/08/serena-williams-still-has-tennis-history-to-make.html

Page 14, line 15: "Mr. Williams Alleges Racism at Tennis Tourney." ABC News. 26 March 2001. 17 Oct. 2016. http://abcnews.go.com/Sports/story?id=99759&page=1

Page 14, line 18: "Williams's Dad Alleges Racism." *The Washington Post*. 27 March 2001. 17 Oct. 2016. https://www.washingtonpost.com/archive/sports/2001/03/27/williamss-dad-alleges-racism/63720e58-1ae9-48e7-8577-da4d4b55dd39/

Page 14, line 22: Chris Chase. "Serena Williams ends Indian Wells boycott, 14 years after racist incident." *USA Today*. 4 Feb. 2015. 17 Oct. 216. http://ftw.usatoday.com/2015/02/serena-williams-end-indian-wells-boycott-14-years-after-racist-incident

Page 16, line 15: Eoghan Macguire and Don Riddell. "Richard Williams: 'I was close to being killed so many times'." CNN. 16 Dec. 2015. 17 Oct. 2016. http://edition.cnn.com/2015/12/16/tennis/richard-williams-venus-serena-tennis/

Page 21, line 5: Larry Schwartz. "Althea Gibson broke barriers." ESPN. 17 Oct. 2016. https://espn.go.com/sportscentury/features/00014035.html

Page 23, line 9: Richard O. Davies. *Sports in American Life: A History*. Malden, Mass.: Wiley-Blackwell, 2012, p. 208.

Page 24, col. 2, line 4: Althea Gibson. USTA. 17 Oct. 2016. https://www.usta.com/About-USTA/Diversity/Black-History-Month/5792_Black_History_Month__Althea_Gibson/

Page 24, line 2: "Althea Gibson broke barriers." https://espn.go.com/sportscentury/features/00014035.html

Page 25, line 5: "Serena Williams motivated by Arthur Ashe." BBC. 26 June 2015. 17 Oct. 2016. http://www.bbc.com/sport/tennis/33282768

Page 25, line 8: Arch Puddington. "Days of Grace, by Arthur Ashe." *Commentary Magazine*. 1 Sept. 1993. 17 Oct. 2016. https://www.commentarymagazine.com/articles/days-of-grace-by-arthur-ashe/

Page 25, line 12: K. Anthony Appiah and Amy Gutmann. *Color Conscious: The Political Morality of Race*. Princeton, N.J.: Princeton University Press, 1996, p. 106.

Page 26, line 1: Matthew C. Whitaker, ed. *Icons of Black America: Breaking Barriers and Crossing Boundaries*. Vol. 1. Santa Barbara, Calif.: Greenwood, 2011, p. 47.

Page 26, line 7: Eric Allen Hall. *Arthur Ashe: Tennis and Justice in the Civil Rights Era*. Baltimore: Johns Hopkins University Press, 2014, p. 31.

Page 27, line 7: William C. Anderson. "Serena Williams' grace helps us escape the banality of racism ... for a while." *The Guardian*. 9 July 2015. 17 Oct. 2016. http://www.theguardian.com/commentisfree/2015/jul/09/serena-williams-grace-banal-racism

Page 28, line 3: "Tennis; The Williams Sisters Have a Date With History."

Page 28, line 8: Interview with Peter Bodo. CNN. 7 July 2003. 17 Oct. 2016. http://transcripts.cnn.com/TRANSCRIPTS/0307/07/lt.03.html

Page 28, line 16: "Richard Williams: 'I was close to being killed so many times'."

Page 29, line 5: John Jeremiah Sullivan. "Venus and Serena Against the World." *The New York Times Magazine*. 23 Aug. 2012. 17 Oct. 2016. http://www.nytimes.com/2012/08/26/magazine/venus-and-serena-against-the-world.html

Page 29, line 10: "Richard Williams: 'I was close to being killed so many times'."

Page 30, line 5: Ibid.

Page 30, line 13: Serena Williams. 17 Oct. 2016. Net Industries. http://sports.jrank.org/pages/5322/Williams-Serena-Born-in-Saginaw-Michigan.html

Page 30, line 19: "Tennis; The Williams Sisters Have a Date With History."

Page 31, line 3: The Wider Image. Mike Blake. Reuters. 17 Oct. 2016. https://widerimage.reuters.com/photographer/mike-blake

Page 32, line 3: Mike Blake.

Page 35, line 9: Robin Finn. "U.S. Open; Little Sister Becomes the Stardust Half." *The New York Times*. 12 Sept. 1999. 17 Oct. 2016. http://www.nytimes.com/1999/09/12/sports/us-open-little-sister-becomes-the-stardust-half.html

Page 36, line 3: "Tennis; The Williams Sisters Have a Date With History."

Page 36, line 28: "Serena Williams Puts Emotion Into Game, Memoir." Morning Edition. NPR. 23 Sept. 2009. 17 Oct. 2016. http://www.npr.org/templates/story/story.php?storyId=113090963

Page 37, line 5: Robin Finn. "Tennis; In Williams vs. Williams, Big Sister Moves Ahead." *The New York Times*. 21 Jan. 1998. 17 Oct. 2016. http://www.nytimes.com/1998/01/21/sports/tennis-in-williams-vs-williams-big-sister-moves-ahead.html

Page 38, line 7: Claudia Rankine. "The Meaning of Serena Williams: On tennis and black excellence." *The New York Times Magazine*. 25 Aug. 2015. 17 Oct. 2016. http://www.nytimes.com/2015/08/30/magazine/the-meaning-of-serena-williams.html?_r=0

Page 38, line 9: Ibid.

Page 38, line 22: Caroline Cheese. "Serena Fulfills promise." BBC Sport. 6 July 2002. 17 Oct. 2016. http://news.bbc.co.uk/sport2/hi/tennis/wimbledon/2106051.stm

Page 38, line 28: "Serena Williams Puts Emotion Into Game, Memoir."

Page 39, line 11: Neil Amdur. "Mrs. King Defeats Riggs, 6-4, 6-3, 6-3, Amid a Circus Atmosphere." *The New York Times*. 21 Sept. 1973, p. 1.

Page 40, line 10: Reuters Reporter and Daily Mail.com Reporter. "'She's the toughest opponent I've ever played in my life.'" *The Daily Mail*. 7 Sept. 2015. 17 Oct. 2016. http://www.dailymail.co.uk/news/article-3225601/Williams-sisters-family-ties-ultimate-test.html

Page 43, line 7: "Serena & Venus Williams win third Olympics tennis doubles gold." BBC. 5 Aug. 2012. 17 Oct. 2016. http://www.bbc.com/sport/olympics/18907509

Page 43, line 15: Harvey Araton. "Williams Sisters Leave an Impact That's Unmatched." *The New York Times*. 27 Aug. 2015. 17 Oct. 2016. http://www.nytimes.com/2015/08/31/sports/tennis/venus-and-serena-williams-have-a-lasting-impact.html?_r=0

Page 43, line 20: Ibid.

Page 43, line 25: Peter Bodo. "Why the Venus-Serena sibling rivalry is different now." ESPN. 7 Sept. 2015. 17 Oct. 2016. http://espn.go.com/tennis/usopen15/story/_/id/13603829/us-open-why-sibling-rivalry-venus-serena-williams-different-now

Page 44, line 7: Rose Minutaglio. "Serena Williams Accepts Sports Illustrated Sportsperson of the Year Award: 'This Only Makes Me Want to Work Harder.'" *People*. 16 Dec. 2015. 17 Oct. 2016. http://www.people.com/article/serena-williams-sports-illustrated-sportsperson-year-speech

Page 44, line 17: Ibid.

Page 45, line 1: "Tennis; The Williams Sisters Have a Date With History."

Page 45, line 7: Mike Blake.

Page 47, line 1: "Williams Sisters Leave an Impact That's Unmatched."

Page 47, line 5: "Women To Serve Up Prime-time Final."

Page 47, line 16: Ben Rothenberg. "Indian Wells Official Quits Post Over His 'Coattails' Remarks on Women." *The New York Times*. 22 March 2016. 17 Oct. 2016. http://www.nytimes.com/2016/03/23/sports/tennis/raymond-moore-quits-tournament-post-over-his-remarks-on-women.html?_r=0

Page 47, line 20: Emily Shapiro. "Serena Williams Fires Back After Tournament Director's 'Offensive' Remarks." ABC News. 21 March 2016. 17 Oct. 2016. http://abcnews.go.com/US/serena-williams-fires-back-tournament-directors-offensive-remarks/story?id=37809182

Page 47, line 28: "Serena Williams' Australian Open outfit brings pop culture to tennis." *Herald Sun*. 23 Jan. 2016. 17 Oct. 2016. http://www.heraldsun.com.au/sport/tennis/serena-williams-australian-open-outfit-brings-pop-culture-to-tennis/news-story/cec4fa4d6d43ce78725abb0c0f84dafd

Page 48, line 3: Ibid.

Page 48, line 11: Christopher Clarey. "It's Time to Appreciate Serena Williams's Greatness." *The New York Times*. 13 July 2015. 17 Oct. 2016. http://www.nytimes.com/2015/07/14/sports/tennis/its-time-to-appreciate-serena-williamss-greatness.html

Page 49, col. 1, line 7: Harvey Araton. "She Stumbled Into Tennis, but Strode Into a Top Post: Katrina Adams Takes Helm of U.S.T.A. After a Long Ascent." *The New York Times*. 16 Jan. 2015. 17 Oct. 2016. http://www.nytimes.com/2015/01/16/sports/tennis/katrina-adams-takes-helm-of-usta-after-a-long-ascent.html

Page 49, col. 1, line 11: Ibid

Page 49, col. 2, line 3: Amy Held. "Advantage Tennis: Improving Game's Racial Disparity." All Things Considered. NPR. 26 Aug. 2012. 17 Oct. 2016. http://www.npr.org/2012/08/26/160070325/advantage-tennis-improving-games-racial-disparity

Page 49, col. 2, line 10: "She Stumbled Into Tennis, but Strode Into a Top Post: Katrina Adams Takes Helm of U.S.T.A. After a Long Ascent."

Page 50, line 2: William C. Rhoden. "Serena Williams Legacy Extends Beyond Grand Slam Bid." *The New York Times*. 12 Sept. 2015. 17 Oct. 2016. http://www.nytimes.com/2015/09/13/sports/tennis/serena-williams-legacy-extends-beyond-grand-slam-bid.html

Page 50, line 12: L. Jon Wertheim. "The Two and Only The French Open removed all doubt: Serena and Venus Williams are in a class by themselves." *Sports Illustrated*. 17 June 2002. 17 Oct. 2016. http://www.si.com/vault/2002/06/17/325325/the-two-and-only-the-french-open-removed-all-doubt-serena-and-venus-williams-are-in-a-class-by-themselves

Page 51, line 3: "Williams Sisters Leave an Impact That's Unmatched."

Page 51, line 5: Felicia R. Lee. "A Documentary Lets the Stories of Black Luminaries Speak for Themselves." *The New York Times*. 23 Aug. 2008. 17 Oct. 2016. http://query.nytimes.com/gst/fullpage.html?res=9F02E1DC1531F930A1575BC0A96E9C8B63&pagewanted=all

Page 51, line 10: Juliet Spies-Gans. "Serena Williams Takes On Body-Shaming Haters In Powerful Speech." *The Huffington Post*. 16 Dec. 2015. 17 Oct. 2016. http://www.huffingtonpost.com/entry/serena-williams-sportsperson-year-ceremony-speech_us_56717235e4b0dfd4bcbffcbf

Page 51, line 16: Serena Williams. "The Ball Is in Your Court." *Wired*. November 2015. 17 Oct. 2016. http://www.wired.com/2015/10/serena-williams-guest-editor-race-gender-equality/

Page 51, line 25: "The Meaning of Serena Williams: On tennis and black excellence."

Page 52, line 2: "Serena Williams Explains Some Aspects of How Racism (White Supremacy) Works." YouTube. 30 Sept. 2011. 17 Oct. 2016. https://www.youtube.com/watch?v=iV_GT5qf-ig&app=desktop

Page 52, line 6: Reeves Wiedeman. "Child's Play." *The New Yorker*. 2 June 2014. 17 Oct. 2016. http://www.newyorker.com/magazine/2014/06/02/childs-play-6

Page 52, line 11: Jone Johnson Lewis. "Althea Gibson Quotes." About Education. 17 Oct. 2016. http://womenshistory.about.com/od/gibsonalthea/a/Althea-Gibson-Quotes.htm

Page 53, line 5: "The Meaning of Serena Williams: On tennis and black excellence."

Page 54, line 8: Ibid.

Page 54, line 12: "Williams Sisters Leave an Impact That's Unmatched."

Page 54, line 19: "Serena Williams: I'm Going Back to Indian Wells." *Time*. 4 Feb. 2015. 17 Oct. 2016. http://time.com/3694659/serena-williams-indian-wells/

Page 55, line 2: Ben Rothenberg. "This Time, Serena Williams Is Cheered as She Leaves Indian Wells." *The New York Times*. 21 March 2015. 17 Oct. 2016. http://www.nytimes.com/2015/03/22/sports/tennis/this-time-serena-williams-is-cheered-as-she-leaves-indian-wells.html

Select Bibliography

Appiah, K. Anthony, and Amy Gutmann. *Color Conscious: The Political Morality of Race.* Princeton, N.J.: Princeton University Press, 1996.

Araton, Harvey. "Williams Sisters Leave an Impact That's Unmatched." *The New York Times.* 27 Aug. 2015. 17 Oct. 2016. http://www.nytimes.com/2015/08/31/sports/tennis/venus-and-serena-williams-have-a-lasting-impact.html?_r=0

Bodo, Peter. "Why the Venus-Serena sibling rivalry is different now." ESPN. 7 Sept. 2015. 17 Oct. 2016. http://espn.go.com/tennis/usopen15/story/_/id/13603829/us-open-why-sibling-rivalry-venus-serena-williams-different-now

Clarey, Christopher. "It's Time to Appreciate Serena Williams's Greatness." *The New York Times.* 13 July 2015. 17 Oct. 2016. http://www.nytimes.com/2015/07/14/sports/tennis/its-time-to-appreciate-serena-williamss-greatness.html

Hall, Eric Allen. *Arthur Ashe: Tennis and Justice in the Civil Rights Era.* Baltimore: Johns Hopkins University Press, 2014.

Held, Amy. "Advantage Tennis: Improving Game's Racial Disparity." All Things Considered. NPR. 26 Aug. 2012. 17 Oct. 2016. http://www.npr.org/2012/08/26/160070325/advantage-tennis-improving-games-racial-disparity

Howley, Kerry. "The Unretiring Serena Williams." *New York Magazine.* 9 Aug. 2015. 17 Oct. 2016. http://nymag.com/thecut/2015/08/serena-williams-still-has-tennis-history-to-make.html

Macguire, Eoghan, and Don Riddell. "Richard Williams: 'I was close to being killed so many times'." CNN. 16 Dec. 2015. 17 Oct. 2016. http://edition.cnn.com/2015/12/16/tennis/richard-williams-venus-serena-tennis/

Puma, Mike. "Venus defeats Serena in 2001 U.S. Open final." ESPN Classic. 8 Sept. 2004. 17 Oct. 2016. http://espn.go.com/classic/s/add_williams_venus_and_serena.html

Rankine, Claudia. "The Meaning of Serena Williams: On tennis and black excellence." *The New York Times Magazine.* 25 Aug. 2015. 17 Oct. 2016. http://www.nytimes.com/2015/08/30/magazine/the-meaning-of-serena-williams.html?_r=0

Rhoden, William C. "Serena Williams Legacy Extends Beyond Grand Slam Bid." *The New York Times.* 12 Sept. 2015. 17 Oct. 2016. http://www.nytimes.com/2015/09/13/sports/tennis/serena-williams-legacy-extends-beyond-grand-slam-bid.html

Roberts, Selena. "Tennis; The Williams Sisters Have a Date With History." *The New York Times.* 8 Sept. 2001. 17 Oct. 2016. http://www.nytimes.com/2001/09/08/sports/tennis-the-williams-sisters-have-a-date-with-history.html

Schwartz, Larry. "Althea Gibson broke barriers." ESPN. 17 Oct. 2016. https://espn.go.com/sportscentury/features/00014035.html

"Serena Williams Puts Emotion Into Game, Memoir." Morning Edition. NPR. 23 Sept. 2009. 17 Oct. 2016. http://www.npr.org/templates/story/story.php?storyId=113090963

Spies-Gans, Juliet. "Serena Williams Takes On Body-Shaming Haters In Powerful Speech." *The Huffington Post.* 16 Dec. 2015. 17 Oct. 2016. http://www.huffingtonpost.com/entry/serena-williams-sportsperson-year-ceremony-speech_us_56717235e4b0dfd4bcbffcbf

Sullivan, John Jeremiah. "Venus and Serena Against the World." *The New York Times Magazine.* 23 Aug. 2012. 17 Oct. 2016. http://www.nytimes.com/2012/08/26/magazine/venus-and-serena-against-the-world.html

Whitaker, Matthew C., ed. *Icons of Black America: Breaking Barriers and Crossing Boundaries.* Vol. 1. Santa Barbara, Calif.: Greenwood, 2011

The Wider Image. Mike Blake. Reuters. 17 Oct. 2016. https://widerimage.reuters.com/photographer/mike-blake

Williams, Serena. "The Ball Is in Your Court." *Wired.* November 2015. 17 Oct. 2016. http://www.wired.com/2015/10/serena-williams-guest-editor-race-gender-equality/

Index

About the Author

As a former teacher, Danielle Smith-Llera taught children to think and write about literature before writing books for them herself. As the spouse of a diplomat, she enjoys living in both Washington, D.C., and overseas in countries such as India, Jamaica, and Romania.